I dedicate this book to my mother, our *Queen*, Denice Brown.

There's not a day that goes by that I do not reminisce on your smile, your words, your motivation, your sense of humor and most of all, the morals and principles you imparted into me. I am because of YOU.

Your only daughter,

Kenya May

Table of Contents

Dedication

Acknowledgement

A Look Inside

Acknowledgements

My sincere thanks to God for sanctioning an incredible, yet unique experience to share with the world.

I couldn't' possibly write a book without honoring my husband, Amere May Sr. since 1995 and my friend since 1989. Together we have been through the some grand moments and he has also been a part of some of the darkest times – poverty, deaths, marriage challenges, parenting, business ventures, dreams, disappointments, betrayal, plans gone wayward, and so many more. Thank you for being my number one supporter.

To my children, Amere Jr., Teaya and Armani, my source of motivation. To my Parents in Love, Walter and Christine Simpson, thank you for countless years of unwavering commitment as I developed from childhood to adulthood. To my siblings, Xavier, Val, Marcus, Nicole, Vernita, and Ashia, thank you for allowing me to share our personal stories with the entire world and encouraging me to dream big. To my aunts, Dorothy, and Tawanna thank you for a constant push towards all of my various goals and ambitions.

Finally, to my supportive church family, Abundant Faith Word Church Charlotte, and close friends for your untiring motivation. You all are aMAYzing!

A Look Inside

Over the years, I've had many people give compliments about how beautiful they think I am. Some people would take it a step further to say "you have such a beautiful spirit". Not knowing that I've not always believed that phrase myself. Looking in the mirror I saw, brokenness.

I've decided to share some personal and painful moments in my life, and I've included them at the beginning of each chapter not necessarily in chronological order. Don't skip over these stories! Read them carefully as they give insight of how and why I am the person I am today. You'll definitely be amazed and inspired. I hope that after this read you will be able to look into the mirror with fresh eyes embracing your own brokenness, your scars, and your flaws; to see that you are *Beautifully Broken.*

Introduction

Appraisals used to be limited to things such as houses, cars, clothing, shoes; you know—tangible things. However, somewhere along the line, we have also started appraising people. We have attached their net worth to their self-worth, and sadly, many believe in this thwarted method of self-evaluation. What is even worse, the people who are doing the judging and assessing, don't even know their value.

There used to be a time where people were loved based on who they were, their character, their personality; but, unfortunately what a person has or doesn't have can determine how they are treated. Too often I run into individuals who have been tossed aside, and abandoned because they seemingly have nothing to offer beyond themselves. Since when were YOU not enough? Since when did the purse you carry have more value than the arm carrying it? Since when did the car you drive have more value than the person driving it? Since when did the houses we live in be considered to have more value than the lives occupying it?

I'm afraid that our society and our world, has gotten it wrong. To our detriment, it is the underlying cause of our broken families, bullying in our schools, the mass incarceration of our youth, the empty chairs in our churches, and the empty seats around our dinner tables. I'm afraid that the careless and selfish disposal of people— mankind— is one of the main causes of the staggering numbers and increase of deaths ruled as suicide. People are starting to believe they aren't worth anything. They're starting to buy into the notion that if one isn't a member of a certain social status, their life has less meaning. Often this is too much for some to handle, and rather than ignore the critics, or wish those who were not afraid to walk away good riddance; they fall into deep depressions that they never recover from. What a sad state of affairs.

Those who do not succumb to suicide usually walk around full of cracks. They know they're broken but rather than fix the cracks, they paint over them, just to cover them up. Many who are broken feel as though there is no use in fixing their cracks because they automatically assume they are going to be broken again. They anticipate the brokenness because they have been broken so many times, and at some point, they get tired of repairing themselves. They grow weary of even caring about the brokenness, and get accustomed to seeing the cracks so much so that they don't even notice them anymore. These are the people who were once high on life, ecstatic about their future, blind to their failures, oblivious to challenges, and had high hopes for their future. But, brokenness changed them. It obliterated their belief that they could accomplish anything they wanted to. Lost somewhere in the abyss of their cracks are their dreams, their goals and their desires. Somewhere, always lurking in the shadows is their total healing but they don't see it. And, they can't see it because of their many cracks.

I hope by the time you turn the last page of this book, you will not only discover that what you have is loosely connected to who you are, but you will be reminded that you do have a purpose, and yes, even broken people can still be used by God.

A Well That Ran Dry...

Growing up in the windy city of Chicago, Illinois, we were like most children, without a care in the world. Our daily routine did not change, we went to school, came home and had a snack until daddy walked in the house at 6:00pm where we sat down to have dinner at the dinner table. If there was a problem at school my brothers, Xavier and Val or my "sister" aunt Nicole would handle it. We could even play outside as long as we were in the house before the street lights came on. I didn't have to worry about anything. To be completely honest, I didn't realize the danger of where we actually lived until I got older.

We would even journey to Mississippi several times a year to visit our grandparents where we played all day and told jokes all night. Best of all, we would leave with caramel cake and fried chicken to eat as we traveled back home.

Life was good and for the most part unchanging, until one day momma decided to stay home from church. Little did I know she was home packing. At the age of 12, my parents separated. At that time I was very naïve believing that things were no different because my parents never argued in front of us, nor spoke ill of each other.

We moved to South Haven, Michigan where my paternal grandmother owned 10 acres of land. The land was plentiful but during that time we only had a trailer with well water. If you know anything about well water there are a number of problems associated with it. From the pressure of the pump, the rusty pipes freezing and the constant need of them being replaced, or the God awful taste of and the shortage of water as the other issues arose. When it was properly working we could only bath and clean with it, leaving both sink and toilet stained from the rust. When it was not working we could rely on two things, water from the springs to cook and drink with and water from the ditch to flush the toilet. Daddy would travel from Chicago to Michigan on Fridays and stay until Sunday evening, making sure he took us to the spring to get fresh water for the week.

Life as I knew it had changed drastically. I felt I like was floating, benumbed as I waited for things to go back to what I knew or thought of as normal. Things like having a two parent home, a house with a dog and cat, those pretty little matching outfits for school, singing in my grandfather's church choir, playing and fighting with my "sister" aunt, no issues, and no concerns.

Meanwhile as time passed, I climbed trees, picked and ate blueberries until I became sick, drove go carts with my brothers, suppressed my feeling, and disconnected from life emotionally. The well, my well, had definitely run dry!

My ability to cope with discomfort of change had increased however, I must admit that the healing was not obtained at this point in my life. I had no idea who I was, what I liked, and why. All I knew is that things were no longer the same.

Chapter One

Brokenness

When I began thinking of writing this book, I knew that I was going to have to take some trips down memory lane to reminisce on my own brokenness. Knowing that, I prayed and asked God to give me the strength and wherewithal to share openly, and transparently, my story and testimony about being broken and being made whole.

I have had many discussions with people about what brokenness really is. The question has always come up as to whether being broken is a positive or negative. Obviously, in our Standard English language, being broken seems to point to a negative connotation. When we refer to people, a broken person often means somebody who has experienced some sort of devastation and they struggle with knowing how to recover or be made whole again. The consequence to most brokenness is the loss of hope and holding on to hope is extremely hard to do when you are broken.

If you read the Word of God, you will discover that anyone who was used by God in a major way was what we could consider as broken. It would take quite some time to navigate through the Bible stories and name those who were greatly tested and broken in their lives and it would take even longer to write how they came out of their brokenness to lead powerful lives. However, in reading about these Biblical heroes of the faith, I have concluded that sometimes you must stop through the land of brokenness to get the lessons needed to help others who too, must face broken times. After all, our purpose in life and the trials and tribulations we go through; are not for us, but for the benefit and blessing of other people.

Brokenness is a process that has no set expiration time associated with it. It tests your faith and endurance and sometimes forces you to question God. Brokenness is a process that we go through and it can take some time for us to understand why but trust and believe there is a purpose for it. Am I saying it is necessary? Yes. How can pain be necessary? Pain is often the prerequisite to the promise. I am sure you have heard the analogy used somewhere before of a woman giving birth. Her pain of labor is necessary for her to birth her baby. Some things make no sense, but when you finally can see what God was working on, you will understand why you had to go through what you went through.

I remember being at one of my lowest points, having a conversation with God. I did not understand how God could sit back and let some of the things I've been through happen to me. It didn't seem fair. It appeared that He had forsaken me. One of the toughest parts about being broken is praying and God responds with silence. There was a time when my self-esteem was low and I was faced with a host of other issues that contributed to my brokenness—all at once. I waited patiently for an audible response and nothing. I was like, "God, are you serious right now?" Just when I needed Him. I've not always done things right but never had I imaged being so broken. I mean, after all, my grandfather was a Pastor, a leader of broken people. I sang in the choir all my life and held a pretty good note, I think. I tried to do everything by the Book. Ever

had or have, those moments where you compared how you were raised

to someone who you KNOW was not raised the same? Better yet, how

you were living to someone who you know was living every kind of way

but Godly? One thing I knew and that was church. You are probably

nodding your head in agreement. I knew church but I was ignorant to the

benefits of Godly living.

The definition of brokenness, in the spiritual sense, is the condition

of being completely subdued and humbled before the Lord and as a

result, completely yielded to and dependent upon Him also.

Psalm 51:17 (NIV) says, "My sacrifice, O God, is a broken spirit; a broken

and contrite spirit, God, you will not despise."

Here is the thing I want you to get very early on, God understands

your brokenness. He is the one person you don't have to pretend with.

You don't have to hide behind your truth, your expensive clothes, your

designer shoes, or your fabulous career. He's the one person who won't look at you in your brokenness and conclude that there's no use for you. Instead, He invites us with open arms to cast our cares upon Him. He wants to take your broken pieces and rebuild something brand new. See, sometimes our brokenness is the prerequisite for our greatest breakthrough. But, I know how difficult it is to trust God through the space between brokenness and breakthrough. I know how difficult it is to go through the process of breakthrough broken. It's like you're trying to enjoy the victory but it's difficult because the victory required so much of you. It took a lot to get it. You lost some stuff trying to declare how great God is and while you're grateful to be able to wave the white flag to signal that you've overcome, you're hurt. Pieces of you are scattered abroad the battlefield.

My mind travels to a particular passage of scripture where a man had to celebrate a victory… broken. Genesis 32:22-32 says, *"That night Jacob got up and took his two wives, his two female servants and his eleven sons and crossed the ford of the Jabbok. After he had sent them across the stream, he sent over all his possessions. So Jacob was left alone, and a man wrestled with him till daybreak. When the man saw that he could not overpower him, he touched the socket of Jacob's hip so that his hip was wrenched as he wrestled with the man. Then the man said, "Let me go, for it is daybreak." But Jacob replied, "I will not let you go unless you bless me." The man asked him, "What is your name?" "Jacob," he answered. Then the man said, "Your name will no longer be Jacob, but Israel, because you have struggled with God and with humans and have overcome." Jacob said, "Please tell me your name." But he replied, "Why do you ask my name?" Then he blessed him there. So Jacob called the place Peniel, saying, "It is because I saw God face to face, and yet my life was spared." The sun rose above him as he passed Peniel, and he was limping because of his hip. Therefore to this day the Israelites do not eat the tendon attached to the socket of the hip, because the socket of Jacob's hip was touched near the tendon." Genesis 32:22-32 NIV*

One of the reasons I want you to admit that you're broken is because your brokenness reflects your tenacity. It is a sign of your perseverance. It is an indication that you've been through some things and have survived. See, a lot of people don't want to admit they are broken because for too long, brokenness has been something bad as something being wrong. NO, my friends. It is the direct opposite. Look at the previous passage. Jacob fought and wrestled all night long for his blessing and was left with a damaged hip. It didn't matter that he was left with a limp. What mattered was that he received his blessing. So, the next time you're tempted to complain, be ashamed of, or embarrassed about your brokenness; just think about what you gained versus what you lost or what was damaged. In Jacob's case, brokenness was a sign of victory. His brokenness was a sign that he was an overcomer. When you can come face to face with adversity and walk away, whether it be limping or crawling, you have reason to shout—to celebrate.

If a poll was taken on each and every person, I think we would discover that not a single person would be able to admit or testify that they have not been broken. Show me a person and I will show you brokenness. I don't care who you are. Everybody has at some point in their life been broken. Crushed. We all know what it feels like to be broken. To get your hopes up, only to be disappointed, to try only to seemingly fail. To believe, only to be slapped in the face and gut punched by doubt. To run, only to get just a little ways before collapsing from fatigue. I know. If you have ever heard me speak, then you know my story. You know the odds that were against me. You know that my life began somewhat broken. Yet, through and by the grace of God, I'm here today able to serve as a witness that no matter how broken and crushed you are, you are still worthy. You are still accounted for among the pieces of your brokenness. If there is a piece, it's still considered usable for something. If there is still a piece of you, you're still YOU.

Let's look at the children of Israel who were greatly broken by disappointment. In Exodus 4:31, the people that Moses led were hopeful concerning their deliverance but when Pharaoh refused to release them they felt some type of way about Moses. Can you really blame them? Hope had been rekindled only to be crushed. But, here's the thing you remember. When it seems all hope is lost, that's the time to put your trust in an almighty God who can do anything but fail. That's the time to anchor down and truly believe that no matter what is happening it is ALL working together for your good. (Romans 8:28) It is the time to place your hope on nothing less than Jesus Christ and His righteousness.

Consider this; think about the type of car you're driving. Should something break on the car would you not be able to take it to the manufacturer and get it repaired? Of course, you would be able to. So, my friends, do you think that your brokenness is beyond repair? Have you tried plugging into the One who made you and knows everything about you? You don't get rid of a car just because it breaks down. You would at least take it in for a diagnostic evaluation before going out to purchase a new one. So, why would you believe that God is going to throw you away just because you're broken? Or that you're of no use because you've got some ripped areas? God forbid! You're of value because even a broken-down car that's not running is still worth something. Often cars run better after they've had a little work done on them and I'm inclined to believe that after you've been broken in some areas, you're going to emerge stronger, wiser and better.

Brothers and sisters, repeat these confessions: "I'm valuable." "God can still use me." "I'm not worthless." "I might be broken but, I'm still here."

See, the enemy wants to keep talking to you as long as you don't talk back. Seeing that he's incapable of telling the truth, his best bet is to feed you with lies in hopes that you won't combat him with the truth. I challenge you to speak the truth today. Declare the word of God over and in your life. Send him and his lies to the pit of hell where he belongs.

And once done, I urge you to walk boldly in your authority, and trust God to take your broken pieces and create something more beautiful than you could ever imagine!

An Insecure Psalmist....

Growing up, I stood in a chair while my mother directed the choir until one day I was able to lead my very own song, "There has been a change in me". I can remember the entire church screaming to cheer me on as sweat ran down my back and I quivered in fright. It is true that as a child I was being "trained in the way that I should go". However, I still needed a change in my mind and in my thought pattern. I lacked confidence in every sense of the word. I was constantly comparing myself to others to the point that I lost sight of my own identity.

It didn't matter that I had my own cheering squad, I had no self-esteem. One of my biggest flaws was the constant need of resembling those in my family. I deemed myself as the black sheep of the family. I had crooked teeth, and nappy hair while those around me had personality, a decent smile, and what some may think of as a decent grade of hair. I did not understand, nor did I appreciate, my individuality.

Nonetheless, as I look back now, I have so many fond memories of my childhood; such as being a daddy's girl and lying across his lap while he pretended to give me milk from his breast as a way to encourage me to drink milk. I can recall wearing five short ponytails to school Monday through Friday until I was old enough to get a "Jheri curl". I stood behind the bedroom door for hours shaking those curls and pretending to be Shirley Caesar. I also remember being the only little girl to wear matching dresses with my mom to church. By golly, I had my very own seamstress!

I think it is safe to say that a significant amount of my broken pieces was a result of me trying to be someone I wasn't. What am I saying? I am saying that we can be the generator for our *Brokenness.*

Chapter Two

Take Me As 1 Am

Mary J. Blige wrote a song entitled, "Take Me As I Am" and the line goes on to say, *"Or have nothing at all."* In other words, you can either like me, love me or leave me. Boy, had I had that mentality growing up I would have spared myself a whole lot of tears and heartache. If I could adhere to the words of the song I sang.

You were created to be unique.

Different.

When it comes to you there should not be a "normal." But, so many have gotten lost in the glaze of society's expectations until they no longer recognize their worth or value. So as soon as someone says something negative about them, or speaks negative to them, they crawl into the shadows; broken by the words of another broken human being. How sad it would be for you to get to the end of your life and discover that you never lived? How sad would it be to get to the end of your life only to have people shake their head in disappointment that you allowed anybody, or anything, to stop you from being all you were designed to be. That would be sad and it would be an atrocity. But unfortunately, people allow the rejection of who they are to determine what they're worth.

Rejection is a feeling no one likes to be a partaker of. Fear of rejection will cause one to forfeit many opportunities, walk away from promising relationships or remain in a state of mental paralysis. Rejection is one of the curses to faith. It prohibits you from having faith because you are too worried about whether someone is going to like you, accept you or validate you. Many of you are not functioning at the level of your highest potential because you're still waiting for someone to clap for you. Your soul is waiting for someone to pat you on the back. I know that when you have been in this area, it is difficult to move beyond it. Rejection not only causes pain, but it causes embarrassment as well. And no one likes to be put to shame. No one likes to feel that their nakedness has been exposed for all the world to see and even if it is not all the world, one person seeing us in a vulnerable state is one person too many.

To reject someone means to refuse to grant that person recognition or acceptance, to discard that individual as being worthless. Have you ever felt rejected?

-Did you feel rejected because your father was distant and cold, too busy to give you time and attention?

-Did you feel rejected because your mother favored an older or younger sibling who was prettier or smarter?

-Did you feel rejected because you weren't gifted in athletics and when the class divided up into teams, you were the last one chosen?

-Did you feel rejected because your school clothes were not as nice as the other kids' and they made fun of you?

Were you fat? Were you plain looking? Did you have acne? Did you have to wear thick glasses? Were you rejected during your high school years because you weren't popular; did you miss your prom because no one invited you? Were you rejected for membership in a sorority you wanted to join in college? Were you passed over for promotion at work because someone else was younger or prettier? Did you lose your job because you were getting older? Did you date a man for several years, expecting to marry him, only to have him back out? Do you feel rejected by your children, after giving your life to raise them and to provide for them the benefits you didn't have? Did your husband leave you in midlife for another woman—or worse yet, another man?

Rejection is a painful experience no matter what the cause and all too often, we don't assign enough blame to the rejector. We simply agree with his or her evaluation of us and carry a feeling of inferiority or of being "damaged goods" all our lives.

REJECTION IS NOT A MEASURE OF TRUE WORTH!

But does rejection really affect our basic worth? If individuals don't appreciate me as a total person because they don't like my looks or my performance, does that mean I really am what they think I am? Am I intrinsically less valuable? Should I permit them to label me for the rest of my life? What if they are wrong?

They usually are.

Let's look at the familiar story of Leah and Rachel. Their story is a prime example of how rejection can disrupt harmony and love in a family. As we study the emotional obstacle of rejection, let's take a look at Leah's spiritual journey, because Leah was a woman who lived with the pain of rejection every day of her life.

First of all, Leah was never respected by her father. In that day, it was the father's responsibility to arrange for his daughters to marry. During the seven years Jacob worked for Rachel, Laban could have tried to find a husband for Leah. If he had offered a big enough dowry, he would have found someone to marry her. But apparently, he thought she was hopeless as a marriage prospect and the only way to get rid of her was to pawn her off on poor Jacob, who was besotted with love for Rachel. Laban passed Leah off to Jacob like a dishonest businessman getting rid of damaged goods at full price.

Leah: Unwanted, Unloved

Can you imagine how Leah must have cringed when Jacob looked at her in the morning light with shock, distaste and anger? That terrible deception on Jacob's wedding night set in motion much of the grief that family experienced for decades to come. Sadly, Leah didn't deserve that rejection. Apparently, her rejection was based on her looks—her weak eyes. Nobody noticed her character, her inner self or her mind. This isn't much different than the way things are today. You've never seen an ugly Miss America, have you?

"Jacob loved Rachel more than Leah". If we think at all about those six little words from Genesis 29:30, we will be able to imagine the many ways Jacob demonstrated his feelings. But we also see how God expressed His feelings for Leah. As we learned in the last chapter, God stepped in to let Leah know she was valuable to Him by allowing her to bear children. Still, Leah suffered her husband's rejection, so from her we can learn some important principles for handling rejection.

FACE THE FACTS REALISTICALLY

Leah knew she wasn't loved. She wasn't fooled and she didn't fool herself. Sometimes we make excuses and cover up for the people who reject us, because if we acknowledge their cruelty, it hurts too much. Worse yet, we keep on trying to be accepted and as a result face rejection over and over.

Leah's longing for Jacob's love probably lasted all her life, but she learned to live with the situation. Her spiritual journey led her to reality and acceptance. Her awareness of God indicates a stable relationship with Him that sustained her and gave her the strength to endure her painful circumstances. Her spiritual growth is reflected in the names she gave her children:

"Leah became pregnant and gave birth to a son. She named him Reuben, for she said, 'It is because the LORD has seen my misery. Surely my husband will love me now" (Gen. 29:32).

Reuben means, "See, a son" but when it is pronounced in Hebrew, it sounds like "He has seen my misery." What does that tell us about Leah's life? She was miserable! Listen to her heart's cry: "Surely my husband will love me now." We learn something important from her.

DON'T PRETEND; CONFESS YOUR FEELINGS

To accept the way things are and to admit you would like them to be different are two different things. It isn't "spiritual" to pretend that everything's fine and you aren't really hurt when you are. Tell the Lord how you feel. He knows it anyway. And, if you can, share your feelings with someone who will pray for you. Both of these honest expressions are important to your emotional and spiritual health.

Despite the birth of Reuben, Leah remained unloved. As the account continues, "She conceived again, and when she gave birth to a son she said, 'Because the LORD heard that I am not loved, he gave me this one too' So she named him Simeon" (Gen. 29:33).

Simeon means, "One who hears." Leah believed that because the Lord had heard that she was not loved, He had given her another son as a consolation prize. What exactly did God hear? Was Leah told in words that she was unloved? By whom? Did Rachel spitefully remind Leah that she was the booby prize as Rachel's jealousy increased because she was barren? Or did this mean that Leah told God in her prayers about her rejection? Sadly, both scenarios were probably true.

Before long, Leah had another son: "Again she conceived, and when she gave birth to a son she said; 'Now at last my husband will become attached to me, because I have borne him three sons.' So, he was named Levi" (Gen. 29:34).

Levi sounds like the word "attached" in Hebrew. This time Leah lowered her expectations. Now she would be satisfied with just some feeling of genuine connection from Jacob and some appreciation. She never mentions love again. It seems she had finally faced the fact that Jacob would probably never love her as he did Rachel.

GIVE UP UNREALISTIC EXPECTATIONS

Sometimes we make ourselves unhappy by envisioning changes that aren't going to take place. Your mother may never be a warm and loving person. Your father may never tell you verbally that he loves you. Your husband may never be able to let down the walls of protection he has built around himself and share the intimacy you long for.

If you spend your life focused on making some other person change, you're wasting your energy. The problem is not yours; the fault does not lie with you. You are not unworthy. Instead, the other person may be incapable of the normal responses of an emotionally healthy person.

We see this happen in Leah when a very important shift occurs in her focus after her fourth son is born: "She conceived again, and when she gave birth to a son she said, 'This time I will praise the LORD!' So, she named him Judah. Then she stopped having children" (Gen. 29:35).

Judah means "praise." After years of pain, Leah's entire focus turned to God. This time she didn't mention Jacob at all; instead she got her sense of worth from God. She knew God valued her because He had proved it to her in a way that was understood in that culture. He gave her children. She was devalued by her father. She was rejected by her husband. She was envied by her sister. But she was loved by God, and that fact gave her the strength to go on.

When we trust Christ, and establish a relationship with Him, He accepts us with arms wide open. His acceptance is what gives us value. It is from Him that we should derive our self-image.

Don't give the person or persons who reject you permission to put a price tag on you. God has put His price tag on you. You are worth so much to Him that He came Himself to die for you so you could be His son or daughter, born into His family by faith in Jesus.

Focusing on God doesn't mean we won't ever feel resentment at unfair treatment. Leah wasn't perfect, either. When Rachel tried to prevent her from having more children by keeping Jacob from sleeping with her, she demeaned herself by "hiring" him for the night with her son's mandrakes. But she also must have prayed, because we read, "God listened to Leah, and she became pregnant and bore Jacob a fifth son. Then Leah said, 'God has rewarded me for giving my maidservants to my husband' So she named him Issachar" (Gen. 30:17-18).

I don't think God gave Leah another son because she gave her maid to Jacob. I believe He answered her prayer simply because He loved her. And even then God wasn't through showering Leah with His blessings: "Then Leah said, 'God has presented me with a precious gift. This time my husband will treat me with honor, because I have borne him six sons' So she named him Zebulun" (Gen. 30:20-21).

When you keep reading, you find out that she was willing to settle for even less—she just wanted her husband to give her the honor due her as the mother of his six sons. As a special blessing, we read that she also gave birth to a daughter, and she named her Dinah. How easy it is to overlook God's blessings because there is something we don't have. Sometimes our "if onlys" blind us to the wonderful provisions we have received, and we refuse to be wholeheartedly grateful.

We will all experience pain in this world if we live long enough. This is a fallen world and we are a fallen race. There's no way to escape suffering. Instead, if we accept it and trust God to use it, He will work it out for our good. God has a way of compensating us for our hurts. And as we learn to deal with adversity, our personal character develops.

Leah was the mother of half of Jacob's sons and half of the twelve tribes of Israel descended from her. Yet she lived with rejection all her life—her father's, her husband's and her sister's. But God proved His acceptance of her in a language she could understand by giving her six sons and a daughter.

Jacob chose Rachel.

God chose Leah.

Rachel had what Leah longed for, but it didn't make her a better person. We see no evidence of contentment or gratitude in Rachel's life. And there is no reason to believe that she had a relationship with the Lord comparable to Leah's. Apparently, the pain of rejection caused Leah to turn to the Lord and in doing so; she found her contentment in Him.

But, no one knows rejection the way our Lord and Savior Jesus Christ knew it.

"He was despised and rejected by men, a man of sorrows, and familiar with suffering. . . . And we esteemed him not" (Isa. 53:3).

Jesus was perfect. There was no sin, no personality or character flaw in Him that caused Him to be rejected. Yet He suffered undeserved rejection all His life. Jesus was rejected by His peers, by His half-brothers, by His nation, by the Gentiles and by the world He had created. In the hour of His agony, He was betrayed by one friend, denied by another and abandoned by all of His disciples. He experienced loneliness, suffering, grief and rejection. "Surely he took up our infirmities and carried our sorrows, yet we considered him stricken by God, smitten by him and afflicted" (Isa. 53:4).

Why did Jesus endure such agony? He bore our sins on the cross and took our punishment so that we might be forgiven. But in so doing He endured a rejection we will never know. He even felt rejected by God, His Father. Remember His cry from the cross, "My God! My God! Why have you forsaken me?" (Matt. 27:46).

When Jesus became man, He bore the full penalty for our sin, which is separation from God: "He was despised and rejected by mankind, a man of suffering, and familiar with pain." (Isa. 53:5).

In the New Testament, we learn more about Jesus' rejection: "He came to that which was his own, but his own did not receive him. Yet to all who received him, to those who believed in his name, he gave the right to become children of God" (John 1:11-12).

Jesus knows how rejection makes us feel. He has been there. He will comfort us, give us value, and use our pain to help others. But to appropriate these gifts, we must make the kinds of decisions Leah did. We must give up our expectations and focus on God, praising and thanking Him for who He is and for the blessings He showers on us. If we do that, rejection will not be a hindrance to our spiritual growth. It will become a catalyst.

A Moment of Truth.....

At the age of 17, my senior year of high school, momma had a come to Jesus moment. She decided to share some truth with me. Two months prior my god-sister who I looked up to lost her father and me being sympathetic called and gave her my condolences. Only to be faced with the moment of truth and told "that's your REAL (biological) father" a couple of months later. I tried to recall who he was, what he might have looked like, when and where I may have possibly seen him and most of all why. How could this be? Could this really be true?

There were thoughts of resemblance and the possibility of having a relationship. If things could have been different had I known earlier, how I can have fixed it, and whether or not it was even worth it? Consequently, I mastered suppressing those thoughts, feelings and emotions; hence everything was of course... all good. I left the house to ride around the town to shed tears alone. I received calls from my brother and "sister" aunt asking if I was okay. Of course the answer was "I'm fine". There was no possible way I could share this empty feeling with anyone. I felt like I was floating, numb, and vulnerable to say the least.

This moment in life affected my psychological disposition. The man I looked to all my life to find resemblance was in fact not responsible for any of my features although he was responsible for my actions as a person. Regardless of this moment of truth, he instilled great values and demonstrated what an absolute GREAT father looks like. Suppressing had become a way of life or so I thought anyway. But, it is true that "all things work together for those who love God" even when you are emotionally *Broken.*

Chapter Three

Vulnerable but Still Valuable

Regardless to the punches life throws our way or how weak they leave us, you must know that there is still purpose for your life. Often it is tough to find the value in your life when you are at your weakest and most vulnerable times.

Almost every single person has dealt with vulnerability and it is a very difficult thing. I can almost guarantee that everyone will agree that no one likes to feel that sort of exposure. But, I'm grateful to those who weren't afraid to show their vulnerability. The people who have opened up in a way that made me feel like it's okay to make mistakes, it's okay to be sad and it's okay to not have the answers to whatever problem it is you're trying to solve. The people who understand that nobody is perfect, that most of us cannot handle, or we get completely engulfed by our pain— those people are the reason why I am able to conjure up the strength to share my painful experiences and embrace the opportunity to do so.

While it is unapologetically easy to fool yourself into thinking you are the only person going through whatever pain you are experiencing. It is imperative that you remind yourself- this experience is not singular to me.

This is not a Public Service Announcement. I am the last person to pretend I know what's good for the masses, let alone myself. But what I do know is that if other people hadn't allowed themselves to open to me, I never would have found the courage to do the same or recognized the value in allowing yourself to be vulnerable.

Vulnerability is often seen as a weakness in life and relationships, but it's a strength. Dr. Brené Brown, a renowned expert on vulnerability, explains that life is best lived when we really "sink into" the joyful moments—daring to show up and let ourselves be seen. She writes,

"When we shut ourselves off from vulnerability, we distance ourselves from the experiences that bring purpose and meaning to our lives."

The dictionary definition of the word vulnerability reads "capable of or susceptible to being emotionally wounded or hurt, as by a weapon" and many who've taken a dip in today's dating pool would agree. The act of opening oneself (physically or emotionally) to another leaves a great possibility of walking away with injuries.

We resist feeling vulnerable because we fear being hurt, rejected or judged by those we want to love. We're scared that after playing all our cards, we still won't be "enough" for said person. In this mindset, many singles try to avoid vulnerability by being numb to feeling altogether. Why get involved in something when you may leave in worse condition than you started, right?

Vulnerability is an important part of self-love because exploring vulnerability allows one to see a greater picture of themselves. Deepening your understanding of vulnerability can be challenging, as it is often hard to face your deepest fears or flaws; but it is important to remember we are only human. By acknowledging your feelings and accepting yourself as you are at this moment, you are giving yourself permission to be vulnerable. Know that this does not mean you are unlovable or undesirable. To be vulnerable is to be strong. It means to stand tall, dressed in your strengths, flaws and experiences and to say "who I am is enough."

Brown advises that it's best "to let ourselves be seen, deeply seen, vulnerably seen; to love with our whole hearts, even though there's no guarantee." If we start with a strong understanding of our own vulnerability and have a sense of self-love, we can live our lives more authentically which creates joy.

Have you ever poured out your heart to someone, only to be met with indifference? Have you ever explained how deeply you love them, only to be told in a cold voice that they don't love you back? We think the solution is to never be that vulnerable again. But God asks us to be this vulnerable all the time — with Him and with others — if we want

true joy. In other words, the thing we think is the worst possible thing, is

the best.

In John 12, we find Mary anointing Jesus' feet with perfume at a

dinner party in front of all the other guests: "The house was filled with

the fragrance." Mary wipes Jesus' feet with her hair. Mary displays the

vulnerability to God to which we are all called.

The Psalms articulate the desperate, honest vulnerable cries for

help that Mary's actions imply. "From the depths of despair, O LORD, I

call for your help." (Psalm 130:1). "I think of God and I moan,

overwhelmed with longing for his help." (Psalm 77:3). "O God, why have

you rejected us so long?" (Psalm 74:1). "Rescue me from the mud; don't

let me sink any deeper." (Psalm 69:14). "I am exhausted from crying for

help; my throat is parched. My eyes are swollen with weeping, waiting

for my God to help me. Those who hate me without cause outnumber

the hairs on my head." (Psalm 69:2-4). "From the ends of the earth, I cry to you for help when my heart is overwhelmed." (Psalm 61:2.) "My heart pounds in my chest. The terror of death assaults me. Fear and trembling overwhelm me, and I can't stop shaking." (Psalm 55:4). "As a deer longs for streams of water, so I long for you, O God. I thirst for God, the living God." (Psalm 42:1-2). "My heart is breaking as I remember how it used to be." (Psalm 42:4). "Why am I so discouraged? Why is my heart so sad?" (Psalm 42:5.) "My heart beats wildly, my strength fails, and I am going blind." (Psalm 38:10.)

David and Mary know the secret to living an abundant life lies in becoming vulnerable to God. Judas criticizes Mary for wasting money that could have been given to the poor, but Jesus praises her for doing "a good thing." See Matthew 26:6-13; Mark 14:3-9; Luke 7:36-50 (it's probable the Luke account is of a different anointing). Jesus had earlier also praised Mary for sitting at his feet listening. She chose the "only thing" necessary, Jesus said (Luke 10:38-42). Similarly, David spent so much time alone with his sheep on the hillside as a young boy that he stormed onto the battlefield armed only with a slingshot because He trusted the "living God" to help him defeat a giant named Goliath. When you spend this kind of time alone with God, you learn that God looks down on humans with love and understanding: "He made their hearts, so he understands everything they do." (Psalm 33:15).

God uses the circumstances of our lives, especially our places of woundedness, brokenness, disappointment and rejection, for good. We are all completely and utterly reliant on God all the time –but we fail to realize this. When bad things happen, we turn to God as David did in the Psalms, with our fears, trembling, despair and brokenness because we have nowhere else to go. We discover no friend, no doctor, no medication can fill the deepest longings of our hearts and so we cry out to the living God and He meets us right there in our place of deepest emptiness. He gives us His strength in place of our weakness. He gives us His love in place of our selfishness. He gives us His joy in place of our despair. He gives us His hope in place of our hopelessness. It's God's nature to give, because He is love. And so that's why being vulnerable feels like the worst thing but is really the best.

We discover our complete reliance on God –and since God is love, we begin to rely on the best thing we could ask for or imagine. When our hearts break, we find God's love right there to mend us. Broken hearts hurt. But that very brokenness that we hate and dread, brings us to a place of such vulnerability that our hearts finally melt with compassion and love when we encounter other people. We stop seeing people as competition to be feared and instead see them as fellow servants of the Living God, who are just as needy, thirsty, hungry and afraid as we are. We can embrace others in love, not needing anything from them, because our hearts are overflowing – our cups runneth over – with the love of God. A love that we find only when everything else in the world fails us. This is abundant living and it's the only way to find joy. When circumstances and other people hurt us and we start to live dependent and vulnerable to God out of our brokenness; we discover that our whole houses become filled with the most expensive perfume of all – the fragrance of God's love.

When we feel like we can't do it, we don't want to be vulnerable, and we're too afraid to trust God – we can remind ourselves that God became completely vulnerable to us. He died naked, abandoned and alone on the cross. Even God turned His back on Jesus on the cross, so that Jesus could experience hell for us. If God didn't scorn the shame of the cross, who are we to be ashamed of anything? Just as the cross is ugly, and yet God transformed it into the most beautiful thing, so our shame, rejection and vulnerability seem ugly to us – and yet if we bring them to the foot of the cross, God can transform our weakest, ugliest and most shameful places into sources of transcendent beauty.

The key to turning your pain into strength is knowing you are more than a conqueror and knowing that God loves you more than you even know. Then, you have to love your way out of hurt and change how you respond to it. Many people experience vulnerability as a result of being hurt but they never get any real healing or closure from it.

I can recall one of the most painful and vulnerable times in my life. It was when I discovered that the man who raised me was not my biological father. What I thought I knew to be true and solid amongst all the uncertainties wasn't. I was crushed. Broken. I was so hurt. Had I found out any sooner I would not have felt any different. The emotional pain and hurt of this particular brokenness was unexplainable.

Unfortunately, no matter how you try to run from the potential of being hurt, it will still find a way to locate you. No one wants to go through life alone, but being broken will convince you that you'd rather be alone that run the risk of being shattered all over again. Thus, the reason I stated that you have to learn how to deal with hurt the proper way. Thwarted views on love only materializes into isolation and depression. Neither of which you can function in life with.

How do you overcome vulnerability and hurt? I'm glad you asked.

Here are some practical steps:

Focus on Blessings

When you're feeling hurt, it's easy to blow things out of proportion and make certain of aspects of your life larger and more important than they should be. You get so caught up in your feelings of hurt that nothing else seems to matter. However, things do matter. In fact, if you take time to think about it, there are probably a lot of things that matter and a lot of things that you can be grateful for.

When feeling hurt, focus on your blessings and on the things you are most grateful for. This will hopefully put your feelings into their proper context. It may even effectively help you re-prioritize and shift your focus onto more important and meaningful things that will bring you greater happiness and fulfillment in the long-run.

Focus on Your Strengths

To find direction during moments of hurt, it's important that you remind yourself of your strengths and the things that have brought you to this point in your life. Your strengths might be your optimism, faith, patience, forgiveness, honesty, compassion, self-belief, etc. These are the things that will get you through this difficult time. In fact, these qualities can help you regain the confidence you need within yourself to move beyond this painful experience.

Therefore it's important to re-direct your energies away from what is hurting you and instead focus-in on your strongest qualities that can help you get through this difficult situation successfully.

Let Go of Past Hurts

Are you holding onto things that hurt you years ago? Maybe you're holding onto these hurts because you feel as though you were unjustly wronged in some way. However, what's the point? Can you do anything about these hurts right here, right now? If you can't, then what's the point of holding onto them? Whatever happened in the past, happened in the past. Let go of these things and move on with your life. This of course doesn't mean that you should forget everything. By all means don't forget these important moments. Learn from them and use them to make better decisions in the present. However don't allow your past hurts to haunt and aggravate the life you're living today.

Smile More Often

Being hurt is a state-of-mind. You are feeling hurt because you are perceiving events, circumstances and people's intentions in a certain way that makes you feel miserable. Is it possible that another person might see things differently? What hurts you might not even phase them. It's all a state-of-mind.

To transform your state-of-mind, try smiling a little more and see how that changes how you feel about the situation. Maybe your feelings of hurt will turn into curiosity. And when this happens, a whole new world of possibilities will open for you.

Always Accept Responsibility

Your pain feels at its worst when you feel as though you had very little control over the situation. You feel as though someone else is to blame and you become the victim of circumstance. This makes you feel powerless and makes it very difficult to move past your feelings of hurt.

One way to instantly feel better about yourself is to accept responsibility for what happened and for how events transpired. In fact, you probably in some way — directly or indirectly — played a part in creating this situation. Recognize this. You are at least partly responsible for what happened and this is a good thing, because with responsibility comes the willingness to make positive changes.

Once you feel at least partly responsible, this gives you the strength you need to potentially make things better — to right the wrongs. You now have the power to mend your relationships and lay down a path for a more positive future.

Surround Yourself with Positive People

One of the best ways to make yourself feel better almost instantly is to talk about your feelings with other people. Have a chat with a close family member or friend and explain what happened. Get their perspective and opinion about the situation, and maybe even work together with them to try and resolve your feelings. There is no telling how much better you will feel once you get things off your chest. Who knows, maybe the other person can convince you there is nothing here that justifies your feelings of hurt. And maybe, that's all you need to help you move forward through this moment of your life.

Don't Take Things Personally

You will always end up feeling hurt if you continue to take things personally. Sometimes people say and do things because they are trying to work through their own personal insecurities and problems. In fact, what they say and do might have very little — if anything — to do with you, and all to do with them and their issues. For this reason, it's important that you step outside yourself during moments of hurt and look at the full picture from their perspective as well as from an outsider's perspective. Maybe this will help you to understand that there is nothing here to feel hurt about. Instead, show a little compassion for the other person and try to help them work through their insecurities.

People Make Mistakes

Sooner or later someone will hurt you. There's no denying this. It will happen. However, often people won't hurt you intentionally. People make mistakes. People make blunders and errors and end up regretting some of the things they do and say. Of course, they might not own up immediately to these mistakes. To do so would wound their pride. What they need is compassion and understanding and maybe a little patience on your part. Eventually they will come around and admit their mistakes, but it might take some time. Be there for them and accept them wholeheartedly, because you might very well be in their shoes at some point in the future.

Learn More about Yourself

Every hurt you experience, gives you an opportunity to learn more about yourself. It gives you an opportunity to learn more about your values, rules and personal expectations. It gives you an opportunity to learn more about others and about how you relate to other people socially and intimately. It gives you insight into people's motives, feelings and intentions. It even helps you get to know yourself and your emotional tendencies at a deeper level. As you learn, you grow and as you grow you will make better choices and decisions in the future that will help you to manage and minimize your feelings of hurt far more effectively.

Guilty but Not Guilty...

It is a fact that having children can be rewarding and filled with excitement and joy. So many precious moments such as birthday celebrations, school pictures, field trips, cute little outfits that don't necessarily match their personality and gifts being opened on Christmas day. Also, living vicariously through them while they play a number of sports; some of which they may or may not be capable of doing. While there are aspects of parenting that are blissful, there are some that are not so rewarding hence they still belong to you. It is true saying that children outgrow your lap but never your heart. I have experienced both special and challenging moments and I wouldn't trade either of them as they have been significant to my developing and maturing in a world of hopelessness.

My oldest child was born my freshman year of college. I had no regrets about bringing him into the world. Looking back in retrospect, I admit that I was not the best parent in the world; but as a young adult I did the best I could. My main focus was making sure that he was fed, clothed, protected, respectful to others and happy. With that being said,

I lacked the ability to understand when too much was not good for the child. In others words, Amere Jr. was spoiled rotten. My support system was phenomenal and enormous which added to this craziness.

As Amere Jr. got older, his love for basketball and music increased along with his longing for social acceptance. However, regardless of what he was told, he was my child that learned through experience. Giving him verbal warnings and instructions just didn't cut it.

One day before school, he asked if he could ride the bus home from school with classmates. Why not, we agreed. After all, it was Friday and the sun was shining in Michigan. Before he proceeded out of the doors he was given specific instructions: "when you get home, change your clothes and make sure that you stay outside with your friends." He verbally agreed and got on the bus. Of course Junior neglected to follow our directions. When he got home he did the exact opposite.

He was guilty of not following directions however he was not guilty of the crime in which they were trying to charge him with.

My eight year old child, along with three other neighborhood boys were being charged with raping an eight year old Caucasian girl. The story goes like this…. Black boys playing with white girl, her father calls home and realizes that there are black boys in the house and he calls the police from his job and makes a claim about his child being raped.

Can you imagine how I felt as a mother? Hopeless to say the least. I didn't know what to do or how to respond.

Not only did I need God, but my child's future depended upon it! I admit that I didn't automatically sing "My hope is built on nothing less, than Jesus blood and righteousness". I lacked hoped and faith during that very moment.

A couple of days later, after taking my child to the police station to be questioned like he was an adult, the phone rang. It was a call to warn me that the incident was placed in the local newspaper. I jumped out of bed and took off running down the street without any shoes to witness this devastation. As I journeyed back which was about half of a mile from our apartment, I searched and searched looking for his name. At the time I was clueless of that fact that minor's names could not be published however I dived back in to the bed and covered my head until morning. Not only did I cry, I stayed there for a few days.

Could this really be?

Will my spoiled, musically talented child be found guilty of such a heinous accusation at the age of eight, even after professing his innocent?

Broken was an understatement!

Chapter Four

Losing Hope

What does one do when they have lost hope and God seems to be silent? What do you do when you are struggling to believe everything you've ever been taught about God? As a believer, one of the worst things ever is to tell other people to put their hope and trust in God, when all hell is breaking loose in your life? How do you offer answers when you are searching for them yourself?

Let's look deeper into what hope is so we can discuss how to get it and hold on to it.

So, hope is used in three senses:

1. A desire for something good in the future,

2. The thing in the future that we desire and,

3. The basis or reason for thinking that our desire may indeed be fulfilled.

Ordinarily, when we express hope, we are expressing uncertainty. But this is NOT the distinctive Biblical meaning of hope. The main thing I want to do is show you from Scripture that Biblical hope is not just a desire for something good in the future but rather, Biblical hope is:

A confident expectation and desire for something good in the future.

Biblical hope not only desires something good for the future; it expects it to happen. And it not only expects it to happen; it is confident that it will happen. There is a moral certainty that the good we expect and desire will be done.

When the Word says, "hope in God," it does not mean, "Cross your fingers." It means, expect great things from God. Hope is something that should not waiver because it is rooted in the faithfulness of God. There should be moral certainty in it because the will and purpose of God are like iron, not chalk.

Here's how I would paraphrase this verse. Wherever there is hope, there is faith. Biblical faith is a confident expectation and desire for good things in the future.

Now faith is the substance of things hoped for, the evidence of things not seen. **Hebrews 11:1**

But faith is more than that …..

You may be reading this book and perhaps thinking that this all sounds good, but Lady May, how can I hope against hope? Meaning, how can I hope when hope has been working against me?

Listen, I know that the times we live in are so full of troubled. People are losing their jobs, a systematic educational system, natural catastrophes and uncertainty in what the future holds. In today's economy, there is little to hope for the future. However, God is never caught off guard or by surprise. God knows the future. You are not the only one that has felt that there is no hope. Even Bible heroes had their n they wanted to give up. Job, Moses, Jonah, Jeremiah and even the powerful prophet of the Old Testament, Elijah. With that said, God will never allow us to suffer beyond our own capabilities to handle it. There is nothing on this earth more certain than hope in God. He will never leave us nor will He ever forsake us. He is our anchor in the present and for the future.

Redemptive Hope

Put your hope in the LORD, for with the LORD is unfailing love and with him is full redemption. **Psalm 130:7**

If you are a believer you can rest assured that God's love is unfailing and He will deliver us in the days of calamity. He has rescued the born-again believer from certain judgment and promised us an eternal home with Him. Instead of using ink, God has signed this redemption with Jesus' own blood which seals you permanently. When our hope is in the Lord and not in ourselves, it is a rock-solid hope.

Gift of Hope

For you have given me hope. Psalm 119:49

We know that there is always hope when we trust in God for He has given us His Holy Spirit to seal us. As we read in Ephesians 1:13, *"And you also were included in Christ when you heard the word of truth, the gospel of your salvation. Having believed, you were marked in him with a seal, the promised Holy Spirit."*

Future Hope

"For I know the plans I have for you, declares the LORD, plans to prosper you and not to harm you, plans to give you hope and a future." **Jeremiah 29:11**

God had plans for you. You can bank on that. His plans are not intended to harm you but to prosper you. Now, this does not mean that He plans to make you rich but He does plan for you to have a secure future. God says that He has plans for you and He knows them even if we do not. Your stockbroker or financial adviser might have plans for you too but they do not know the future. They may try to plan for a secure future but they do not have the ability to bring it about. God knows your future and is planning it better than anyone else can, even you.

Unending Hope

*Put your hope in the LORD both now and forevermore. **Psalm 131:3***

Hope is for now, it is for today and it is for tomorrow too. Jesus clearly tells Christians that He will never leave us, never forsake us and will never, ever cast us away (John 6:37). This promise is for tomorrow morning, next week and next year. This hope is the believer's hope that covers their entire life. It is without end and will stay with us until Jesus comes for us.

Lovely Hope

*The LORD delights in those who fear him, who put their hope in his unfailing love. **Psalm 147:11***

I am a mother and grandmother. My children have troubles. They come to me for advice. I am always offering them hope that all things will work out for their best, despite what today may seem like (Romans 8:28). I delight when they come to me with their troubles. So too, does the Lord delight when we put our hope in Him and His unfailing love. He wants us to depend upon Him for everything. He delights to give us the desires of our hearts (Psalm 37:4).

Unashamed Hope

*No one whose hope is in you will ever be put to shame… **Psalm 25:3***

If we have our hope in the right place that is not in ourselves, our jobs, our circumstances, but in God alone we will never be disappointed. We will never be ashamed for placing our hope in Him because He has the power to deliver us out of all our troubles. We do not possess that power. Our 401K does not have such power. God owns the whole earth, He owns every animal in the forest, and He is the owner of the cattle on a thousand hills as Psalm 50:10-11 says, *"for every animal of the forest is* mine, and the cattle on a thousand hills. I know every bird in the mountains, and the insects in the fields are mine."

Guiding Hope

*Guide me in your truth and teach me, for you are God my Savior, and my hope is in you all day long. **Psalm 25:5***

We are finite creatures and cannot look beyond today but God has planned every step we take. He guides us and protects us, even in areas where the dark shadows of death seem imminent in the lowest valleys (Psalm 23). We might plan our own course but God Himself determines where our steps go (Proverbs 16:9).

Courageous Hope

*Be strong and take heart, all you who hope in the LORD. **Psalm 31:24***

If we are not a believer, then we only have hope in this world, among men and are most miserable. But if we are Christians, then we can take heart and be courageous because God is our hope. When God is your hope you have a sure thing. When it is in the world, then we are consumed with worry because we don't know what comes next. Those who have hope in God have hope in the only One who can guarantee our future.

Reverent Hope

But the eyes of the LORD are on those who fear him, on those whose hope is in his unfailing love, **Psalm 33:18**

When we hear the words "fear in the Lord" or "those who fear him" this is not a fear of punishment or retribution. Fear is simply a reverential respect and standing in awe of God. That is what "fear of the Lord" means. It means that those who reverence God and His name have nothing to fear at all; no evil, no pestilence, no begging for bread and no fear of want. His unfailing love is upon those that fear or revere Him: His love never fails and His eyes are fixed on you. You are the apple of His eye (Deuteronomy 32:10, Zechariah 2:8).

Protective Hope

We wait in hope for the LORD; he is our help and our shield. **Psalm 33:20**

Our hope in God is a shield of life. Not only a shield in eternal life but in the present life. He is our help when we need it and our shield when we need protecting. God alone is our help and our shield.

Sovereign Hope

But now, Lord, what do I look for? My hope is in you. **Psalm 39:7**

When we look to ourselves, our employer, our retirement fund or our inheritance, we cannot fully hope with 100% certainty. But what do we look for when our Hope is in God? We know that even our employer's decisions are in God's sovereign hands. Proverbs 21:1 says, *"The king's heart is like channels of water in the hand of the LORD; He turns it wherever He wishes."* The king thinks he might be in charge, or the boss might think he or she is making their own decision, but in God's sovereignty, they do nothing that is not in God's divine plan for us. They are subject to the Lord's will whether they know it or not.

Praise Worthy Hope

Why are you downcast, O my soul? Why so disturbed within me? Put your hope in God, for I will yet praise him, my Savior and my God. **Psalm 42:11**

(These are repeated in Psalm 42:5 and Psalm 43:5)

Here the Psalmist examines his own heart in asking, why am I so downcast? Why am I so disturbed? When really, he has no reason to be because when hope is in God we have reason to praise our Savior and our God. If you do not know Christ, then I would agree that there is every good reason to be downcast, to be depressed and to be so disturbed. The world is a most uncertain place to live in today, far above any other day but, not so for those whose hope is in God.

Restful Hope

Find rest, O my soul, in God alone; my hope comes from him. **Psalm 62:5**

I have often times wrestled with tomorrow while I lay down to sleep. The many "what if's" haunt my mind and do not allow me to sleep as I rehearse the day's events and worry about what happens tomorrow if... But worrying about tomorrow is borrowing trouble from tomorrow and spending it on today. When you realize that tomorrow is already taken care of by God alone and the hope you have in Him, then you can find rest. It is easier to sleep tonight if you know tomorrow is in God's hands.

Now, let's look into losing hope from a practical perspective and discuss ways you can renew hope.

As we have already gone over, hope is the life force that keeps us going and gives us something to live for. Hope is a crucial part of dealing with life's problems and maintaining resilience is the face of obstacles.

Even a glimmer of hope that our situation will turn around can keep us going.

When we begin to lose hope, things can seem bleak. When we run into constant resistance and are prevented from reaching our goals we can start to feel like there is nothing to live for. If we can't get to where we want to be and don't feel in control of our life, what's the point?

If you or someone else is feeling apathetic and are tired of running the rat race of life you may be starting to lose hope. To open new and fulfilling possibilities for your future, you may need to nurture hope.

How we lose hope

- *Lacking hope from the beginning* – If we experienced neglect and were never nourished as a child, we may never have developed a healthy level of hopeful thinking. We might not have confidence and resilience set in place, and simply struggle when things prevent us from achieving our goals.

- *Loss of connections* – When we experience loss over time we can start to feel hopeless. Loss can come from divorce, death and change. We can also experience loss of intangibles like a job or other important aspects of our identity. When we hold on and wallow in our grief from these losses, hopelessness can set in.

- *Victimization* – When we are abused and belittled we can start to believe that is how life is supposed to be. We can begin to feel that we don't have any control over what happens to us and that bad things will always occur. This can relate to unfair treatment from prejudice and discrimination.

- *Burnout* – If we don't take care of ourselves we can get exhausted and overwhelmed to a point where life seems to run over us. We no longer feel able to manage our responsibilities and develop a negative and cynical view of the world and others. Burnout can lead us to feel defeated.

How to Renew Hope

In much of the research examining hope, a major factor that contributes to our level of hope is the achievement of our goals. When we are able to reach our goals, and have a sense of support and validation it instills hope.

In this sense, empowering yourself by setting effective goals is the key. Here are a few tips to set and achieve your goals and bring more hope into your life:

Prioritize goals

There are so many areas in life that we may like to see improvement, but we can't do everything at once. So, figure out what domains of life you want to achieve goals in and what's most important between these. Do you want to have better relationships, get a job or have better physical health? Pick one area to begin and set a realistic goal that you will be able to achieve.

Set SMART Goals

In order for goals to uplift and enliven us we need goals that are challenging and motivating yet are still realistic. A good acronym to follow in order for goals to be effective is "SMART."

- **S**pecific

- **M**easurable

- **A**ction oriented

- **R**ealistic

- **T**ime bound

Move Past Barriers

When working toward our goals there's likely to be some unexpected situations that occur. We need to be ready to deal with obstacles and drawbacks. Consider what barrier you could run into and how to be prepared to manage it. When they arise, you will be ready, have a plan and won't be able to use this as an excuse to give up. It will also be an important aid to the success of your goals.

We need to know where we're going and have an idea of how and when we're going to get there. By achieving small steps along the way, you can renew hope and continue to stretch yourself further. When we break down goals into short-term, mid-term and long-term expectations it provides clear direction and measurable progress that can keep us motivated and hopeful for a successful future.

I hope this chapter has been a blessing to you. In a political climate where it seems as if our country has lost all hope in the newly elected President, now is a good time to renew our faith in God and hope for a future that will benefit us in the most positive way. It is my prayer that you take away from this chapter the importance of holding on to hope. Somebody is counting on you to not give up. Somebody is watching how you deal with trouble and the storms of life when they arise and they are patterning themselves after you. So, regardless as to what you are going through or what you may be facing, giving up is not an option. Defeat is not an option. Throwing in the towel is simply NOT an option.

When you find yourself getting weak in the faith and possibly experiencing hope fading away into the distance, I've included some Bible verses below to help strengthen you.

Hope on my brother and my sister!

Hope In God Bible Verses:

If you are feeling hopeless and worried about tomorrow, next week or even next year read the rest of these verses and see how far having hope in God goes:

Psalm 65:5 *You answer us with awesome deeds of righteousness, O God our Savior, the hope of all the ends of the earth and of the farthest seas*

Psalm 69:6 *May those who hope in you not be disgraced because of me, O Lord...*

Psalm 71:14 *But as for me, I will always have hope; I will praise you more and more.*

Psalm 71:5 *For you have been my hope, O Sovereign LORD, my confidence since my youth.*

Psalm 9:18 *But the needy will not always be forgotten, nor the hope of the afflicted ever perish.*

Romans 12:12 *Be joyful in hope, patient in affliction, faithful in prayer.*

Psalm 9:18 *But the needy will not always be forgotten, nor the hope of the afflicted ever perish.*

Job 11:18 *You will be secure, because there is hope; you will look about you and take your rest in safety.*

Psalm 33:18 *But the eyes of the LORD are on those who fear him, on those whose hope is in his unfailing love.*

Psalm 33:22 May *your unfailing love rest upon us, O LORD, even as we put our hope in you.*

Psalm 119:74 May *those who fear you rejoice when they see me, for I have put my hope in your word.*

A Personal Invitation to the Trailer...

The cute drummer from church swept me off my feet. He had a personal invitation to my house whenever he wanted. He spoke kind words to me, he overlooked my crooked teeth and toes, along with the smell of kerosene. He did everything within his power at that time to make sure that I felt socially accepted and I didn't have feelings of rejection and above all, I was his main thang.

I dated and eventually married my childhood sweetheart at the age of 23. No, not every day was peachy cream but we believed that we were doing the right thing, being that we were born and raised in church and both of our grandfathers were pastors. Not to mention, our first child was already born and headed to primary school in couple of years. With hopes of making some positive moves for the entire family we decided to move to North Carolina where my husband was offered an opportunity to play basketball again.

After getting settled in the great southern state, our move had great hopes of becoming something positive until one day he picked me up from work with a strange look on his face. We stopped by the church to talk with our new found pastor followed by having a quick dinner. I had plans with some of the young ladies from the church. After returning home to freshen up, he came into the bathroom to make small talk, at least that's what I thought. I continued putting on make-up and he finally made the statement, "I really have something to share with you". "Go ahead", I pleaded because whatever it was, it would not stop me from going out with the girls. As I put on the finishing touch of my lipstick to match the fire-red pants suit I was wearing, he opened his mouth and ruined the entire night. "I've had an affair and she had a child, TODAY"........

One form of bondage that I previously managed to master was to pick up the pieces and keep it moving regardless of how it made me feel.

As my girlfriend pulled into the driveway and blew the horn, I looked into the eyes of the only man I had ever been with and asked one simple question; "Is that all you needed to say?" While he waited for dramatic response, I did what I knew best. Kept a straight face and kept it moving. Of course he followed me to the car but it wasn't until I pulled off that the tears began to flow. Brokenness was an absolute understatement at that time. I left the house shattered, with thoughts of whether I should take a drink or break all the windows out the car. But, neither of the two options made sense.

I proceeded with the night, not remembering anything or anyone but one thing's for sure, my heart was broken. *Broken* by infidelity and most of all, *broken* by truth.

Chapter Five

Rejected to be Redirected

In a previous chapter, we talked about rejection and the devastating effects it can have on someone's life. In this chapter, I want to share with you the blessing that being rejected can have on your life.

Most people can't see that being rejected can be a blessing, but that is because sometimes we fail to realize that rejection can often be a sign of God's redirection.

Looking back, I realize that God was protecting me. At the time, I didn't view it as such.

However, I felt the deepest sense of rejection ever, and I was a wreck. It took a while for me to come to terms with everything going on around me and come to a place where I completely sought God to pull me out of my emotional mess. But, God pulled me out of my emotional mess and He redirected me. I developed a daily time of prayer where

God met me and delivered me from not only brokenness but an unexplainable peace concerning both husband and child. Now, I am a proud mother of three children, two of which I bore and a girl I never had.

This had nothing to do with me. Honestly, looking back, I am glad it happened. Had it not, I wouldn't have learned how to forgive, how to be strong when life was trying to take me out and I even learned what it meant to be a better me through the power of Christ.

It takes more than the power of feelings to overcome rejection. It takes the power of God.

Rejection isn't so bad when we stop and realize *why* we are rejected. Most of the time when we are rejected it is either fear of the other person or it simply just isn't the right person or the right time.

Everything is in God's timing.

If you have ever been rejected, know that it has nothing to do with you and everything to do with God's plan for your life.

God is protecting you - let Him.

Psalm 91

Whoever dwells in the shelter of the Most High will rest in the shadow of the Almighty. [2] I will say of the LORD, "He is my refuge and my fortress, my God, in whom I trust."

When someone rejects you it's just God's way of saying, *"I have something better in mind for you; you just have to wait a bit longer and don't lose hope."*

We have all been rejected at some point in our lives and I want to tell you congratulations! You may be asking yourself why this woman is congratulating me on being rejected. Well you see, rejection doesn't necessarily mean that you have failed or that you are not good enough. Rejection happens to give you a wakeup call to change the direction that you are going. As I have said and will say again and again, rejection is simply God's protection.

I know what you might be thinking, how can rejection be protection, because when you are being rejected it doesn't feel like any protection is going on in that moment. Being rejected can feel downright frustrating, disappointing and many times you feel like a complete failure. I totally hear you on this and as humans these are our first responses and emotions that come up when we are dealing with being rejected. However, when we are rejected in one way or another it is really the best thing that can ever happen to us. We might not think so initially, but when we look back at the situation we can always see an opportunity. So, if you are stuck in contributing to your own "rejection pity party," I want you to stop and ask yourself what are some of the opportunities in your current "rejection" situation. Once you have made the decision that you want to find the opportunity in your situation, your thinking will automatically start to shift and this will help you to move forward.

The next step is to create a mantra that will help to support your new way of thinking. One great mantra that I use is, "If not this, then something or someone so much better is on its way." Creating this new thought and mantra is so important because it literally shifts your mood, your energy and makes space for something even better to come along. You must trust and believe you are being supported in every moment of your life by a higher power. You were not created in this lifetime to become a failure; you were created to become a total success in life and this I know for sure.

It is your birthright to be successful and to experience unlimited health, wealth and abundance in every aspect in your life. While at times you might not feel abundant you must trust that you are exactly where you are supposed to be and that you are well on your way to living the life you have always wanted. There are many times in my own life that I look back and I am so thankful that I got rejected; whether it was not getting a job that I so desperately wanted or getting denied for a loan that I so desperately needed. In every situation that I was "rejected" something else or someone else came into my life that was so much better!

We are all here to learn and grow from our life experiences. If you are currently going through being rejected or want to be able to handle any kind of rejection that might come your way in the future I have summarized the **3 steps on how to handle rejection with more ease:**

1. Feel the Funk – I want you to feel those initial feelings that come up when you experience any sort of rejection. Do not deny any of your feelings. It is so important to feel your initial feelings, acknowledge them and release them physically. Releasing these emotions could mean going out for a run, taking a boxing class, jumping on a trampoline or writing. Whatever way you do this, you want to make sure you acknowledge and feel your feelings that come up first and then release them out of your body and back into the Universe.

2. Shift Your Thoughts – Your thoughts are very powerful! After you have felt your initial feelings and physically released them, I want you to shift your mindset and start to become thankful for being rejected and know that something or someone even better is on the way. Every time you think about the situation I want you to say the mantra "if not this, then something or someone else so much better is on the way for me."

3. Trust and Believe – Really trust and believe this new mantra. Try to embody and accept this as truth in your life as much as you can. Trust and believe that God is at work for you and will give you a sense of relief. Everything is working for you, not against you. (Romans 8:28)

Our ability to see the full scope of our lives and God's plan is amazingly limited. As Paul says, "we see through a glass darkly but will one day see Him face to face" (1 Corinthians 13:12). Because of our limited view, we often do not see that the failures and disappointments we face are nothing other than God's redirection of our lives to those places where He can use us the most.

Consider Moses who failed at being an Egyptian prince so God could use him to lead the people out of bondage. Or, Joseph who failed at being a brother so that he could save his whole family from famine. My greatest perceived failure brought me to where I am today and right where I believe God wants me to be. As the book of Proverbs says, "In their hearts humans plan their course, but the Lord establishes their steps" (Proverbs 16:9). How often God has redirected my steps in ways that I did not understand at the time but in retrospect I have more clarity.

This ought to cause us to ask in failure and disappointment, "Is God up to something?" "Does He have something in mind that is greater than our disappointment?" Since He establishes our steps and has our best interests in mind, chances are He does. This allows us to change our prayer from "why?" to "What?" Obviously, God has something different for us than we expected. The question is, "what is it"? Asking *why* keeps us focused on our disappointment while asking *what* focuses on God's intentions and what He has for us next. Two very different perspectives that lead to two very different attitudes.

Here is something we know for sure: God is always up to something, even in our failures and disappointments. We are never abandoned or left alone so even in the worst place we can look with anticipation at what He has for us. This truth gives us the courage to move forward even in dark days. We know He is up to something, we just don't know what - yet!

Life without You...

Life altering moments can make you better or bitter.

I had hopes of daddy selling his house and moving to Michigan with me. The thought of him going to the kid's basketball games with popcorn in his dentures, coming home to a prepared southern cooked meal, planning and maintaining a garden in the backyard and so many more were ideal but things just didn't pan out that way.

I received a call from daddy stating that he couldn't get out of the car. I call his next door neighbor and they headed straight to the hospital. Subsequently, a couple of days turn into twenty-six only to find out that he had aggressive cancer in three major organs. I remember the day of surgery, I reached out to say once last prayer and he responded by saying "we are not going to keep bother that man (God) about the same thing," although he gave me specific instructions to carry out if things had gone wrong. .

During this twenty six day transition, I was taunted with the thought of should I share with him that he in fact isn't my biological father, did he know already know this information, did he even care, how different things would have been, the denial of maybe there were resemblance, and so many more.

With all these questions going through my mind I can remember suppressing every emotional feeling and pretending that everything was okay. After all, I had a job to do, I had orders to follow and there was no time for emotions, reactions or grief.

The time had come and after hoping and praying day in and day out, after being accused of not giving him enough time to bounce back before pulling the plug, after being attacked by a particular relative for material items, and approached by his significant other about property and deeds, I was asked one question. What do you want? My answer still remains today "I want my daddy here with me". Not only was he gone but I was an emotional wreck, *Broken.*

Chapter Six

Abandoned but Not Forsaken

Abandonment is something I wish I could not identify with and actually did not experience until the loss of my parents as an adult. However, there are so many people from birth, and many years throughout their life, have to deal with abandonment. People walking away. Sometimes without giving an explanation or reason, they just walked away. Of course, this leaves a void and an emptiness that isn't easily filled. Depending on who abandoned you, it can be tough to recover. It leaves you broken, scarred and the hole they leave gets bigger every day they are away.

I pray that the nuggets of wisdom that I offer in this segment helps you in dealing with abandonment.

First, in order to move on from abandonment, you have to refrain from over generalizing things. Fear does that to us. It makes us overgeneralize a possible threat.

"I was left by my husband! - No men can be trusted!"

"I was cheated on by my wife! - I can't trust any women."

"Someone I love left me! - Never allow yourself to love because you'll always be hurt!"

This over-generalizing prevents people trusting and truly committing to all kinds of different relationships. Because people and circumstances *are* different and until we can *feel* the difference, we'll condemn ourselves to needlessly unhappy lives.

Really start to focus on the *differences* between people and circumstances. When we are frightened, we avoid. This is natural, but if we are frightened of what we need then this avoidance makes us unhappy. Everybody and everything will not yield the same results. Yes, the color black can represent darkness, but in fashion it represents a slimming effect. Same color, but serves different purposes. Everyone isn't going to leave you. Everyone won't hurt you.

Next, you have to sort out of the past.

If you are solution-focused, dwelling on the past, digging through old hurts, trying to "get to the root of it all" isn't appealing to you. So often, that doesn't help beyond giving someone a sense of why they feel bad; it doesn't help them see how they can move on.

Of course, sometimes the past does keep tripping up the present, so we need to do something. But it's not enough just to "explore" what happened. We need to change the way it feels so it can stop bothering us.

If you experienced abandonment as a child, your mind may have deduced that if a parent left you, then friends, romantic partners and other significant people in your life are bound to leave you as well. If you took this loss personally and somehow felt responsible for your parent leaving you, then you may feel like your parent chose to leave because you weren't worthy enough for him or her to stay. Clearly, these deductions are fallacious. Human beings undergo complex psychological processes -- making all sorts of choices -- and children aren't responsible for a parent's choice to abandon them. If you believe that you're worthless, then all your actions will be in line with that belief. You need to realize that you're not to blame for your parent's abandonment and see yourself as worthy of love and healthy relationships.

Another key to dealing with abandonment is to redirect negative thoughts. Yes, prepare for the worst and then...forget about it. Often when people are abandoned (whether because someone leaves or even dies), they feel utterly hopeless and helpless. But you are never helpless. The Lord promises to never leave or forsake us.

Write down a list of all your personal strengths, attributes and character traits that would get you through if you were to be abandoned. Next write down a list of people and outside resources that would help you "survive". Even take some time to imagine how you'd cope, then thrive. When you stop thinking of yourself as hopeless and helpless, you stop feeling so vulnerable and you start enjoying your life more. Does this mean you should pretend as though their leaving or dying didn't hurt? Of course, not. But instead of focusing on their departure, begin to get excited about the arrival of new people in your life. Sometimes people have to go, for others to come.

Understanding the Signs of Abandonment

1. Physical or emotional abandonment most often results in low self-image, because we ask what was wrong with us, that the other person, especially our parents, did not want a relationship with us.

2. If we have been abandoned by our fathers, we will usually rebel against the authority figures in our lives because we feel that we cannot trust anyone except ourselves.

3. Once we have experienced abandonment, we may expect that others might also abandon us since we feel unworthy of their love.

4. Because the emotional pain of feeling worthless is so great, we will many times abandon or show contempt for others that we are afraid will abandon us. This results in additional experiences of abandonment.

Steps for Overcoming Feelings of Abandonment

1. Remember; never question the behavior of others which you have no control over. You are only responsible for YOU!

2. Establishing a close, intimate relationship with God is the answer for overcoming abandonment, because He alone can be trusted completely to look out for us and never leave or forsake us. We must make a covenant with Him.

3. If possible, we must work through our issues of low self-image and our feelings of abandonment with those who have abandoned us in order to be completely free from this fear.

4. If we will do this, we can be set free from this trap and go on to experience a long and full life.

Pain that Built Walls...

Every Sunday I had the privilege of riding to church with my grandpa listening to his sermons before he actually delivered it to the people. At the time, I thought it was comical. I had no idea of God's plan for my life to be connected and married to a preacher even today. On any given day it is not unusual for us to debate and share the word of God prior to Sunday worship. Although I was familiar with the amount of responsibilities a pastor faced, I never equated leadership to pain......Furthermore, I surely didn't want to be the person that endured the pain.

Early on in ministry, I did what most naive leaders do. I extended my arms and trusted a young lady into my home and around my children. This relationship was rewarding as she ran errands as need, seen about my children and helped around the house. I made sure not to take advantage of her by paying her for her services and keeping the relationship honorable as we also lead her to Christ.

One day while doing a check and balance on our bank statement I noticed that there were more transactions than I had authorized. This young lady had been writing and cashing checks from our account. Not only did she benefit financially she admitted to talking negative about us to various members of the church. Eventually she moved to another state by walking away from the church, the family and my children without an apology or rectifying her behavior.

I have learned over the years that no matter how hard you try avoid hardship within ministry it's inevitable. From betrayal, to being misunderstood, criticized, taken advantage of, disrespected, etc. there is no getting around it. After hitting my head a few times I built a wall. After all, I was not the head Pastor. I could go to church, cross my legs, sing a few songs, and go home with my family. This wall created a guarded place, boundaries for the people we served but it also created a space of loneliness and a number of trust challenges.

Chapter Seven

Picking up the Pieces

"Never look back unless you are planning on going that way." ~*Henry David Thoreau*

When you have been broken, you must believe that you are in the prime position to create something new, something beautiful.

As you begin to focus on picking up the pieces of what's been broken, one of the first things you should do is learn how to live in the present. It is merely impossible to be in the present while being in the past. You must make a choice. The past is never going to relinquish you to your present without putting up a fight. The past knows that if you ever break free from it, there will be no limits to what your future can be. To the contrary, if it can hold on to you long enough, it will have you forfeiting your future before your future can show you what it's capable of.

Focusing on the present moment is something I and a lot of other people, struggle with daily. That's just being transparent. Hard as you try, as much as we know it's so much better to live in the now; we struggle with finding the present moment among our constantly racing thoughts. Whether it's the already-happened past creeping back into our mind or the who-knows-if-it-will-happen future taking hold of my thoughts. Often we find ourselves living somewhere other than the present moment. And of course, that's not what we want to be doing.

Looking backward at times can be the fault of mine -- and in fact, was one of the reasons I wrote this book. I wanted to -- and still want to -- stop focusing on the past. Whether it's getting married too young, handling family issues differently, how different things would have been, or the mistake of having my first born at an early age. All of the possible mishaps seem to find their way into my mind, clearly hindering my ability to live fully in the present moment. Like most people, thoughts of the past impact my present -- and not often in a positive way.

But, there are some things I'm learning to put into practice as I focus on living in the NOW. The first thing is: don't believe everything you think. Listen, sometimes you can't trust your thoughts. Your mind will formulate all sorts of things if you aren't careful. The same way we are given God-like, supernatural thoughts, the enemy manages to implant a few as well. But, you have to always remember that the enemy is not capable of telling the truth. So, you can always determine what's from him by fact checking it with the Word of God. If it is in contradiction to what the Word declares, it's from the enemy and cannot be trusted or believed.

The next thing is to forgive everyone who hurt you in the past. Unforgiveness is the chain that binds us to our past and prohibits us from moving on. You've got to let it go and GO. Don't miss that. I'll say it again, let it go and GO! In other words, let what they did go, let who hurt you go and then you GO on with your life. It's over. Yes, it's tempting to hang around to see if a moment will present itself for you to get revenge. But vengeance is the Lord's, and I promise you that what He can do is far better than anything you can conjure up.

The Bible says in Philippians 4:13, "Brethren, I count not myself to have apprehended it, but this one thing I do: forgetting those things which are behind, and reaching forth unto those things which are before." Sometimes moving on feels like leaving a piece of yourself behind. Other times forgetting those things which are behind seems like an exercise in futility. Still other times reaching forward to those things which are ahead is well, let's just say you may feel there is a tug of war in your soul threatening to tear you apart.

Again, I know that pain all too well as I have experienced it a number of times.

Forgetting those things which are behind is perhaps one of the greatest challenges we can face, especially when those "things" were a major part of our daily lives. I've had to "forget" a loved one, people who

I deemed a friend, hiccups while doing ministries —and sometimes in the midst of great persecution.

But I'm here to tell you that we can forget those things which are behind. Or at least we can remember them without the gut-wrenching pain we felt while we were making the transition. And we can press on toward the goal with joy.

I had to quickly grab hold of the reigns of my mind, stop replaying the scenes over and over again in my soul and reach forward to those things which were ahead. The only way out is through, and it starts with a disciplined mind.

Maybe for you it's not a relationship, per se. Maybe you need to forget past hurts, past failures—or even past successes. The point is this: Dwelling on an unpleasant past, no matter how recent or far away that past is, can't lead to healing. Dwelling on an unpleasant past isn't the path to forgiveness. Dwelling on an unpleasant past can't send you to the next place God wants to take you. It just can't. Dwelling on an unpleasant past can only keep you tied to that past, which hinders you from moving forward in God.

Beloved, if you were led by the Spirit of God to end your relationship with a person or place or if the enemy caused you to experience great loss in your life through death, divorce or some other tragedy, God has something better for you. If your past is one of shame, guilt and condemnation for sins you have committed, God is ready, willing and able to forgive you and cleanse you from all unrighteousness (1 John 1:9).

Friends, simply put; trust God to help you pick up the pieces. He will restore anything the enemy stole from your life—and He may even restore relationships with people who walked away from you (or people He told you to walk away from). Our job is not to wonder what could have been or what will be. Our job is to obey God. Be assured, when we don't walk in obedience to the Word, the challenge to forget those things which are behind becomes even greater. He gives grace to those who seek to obey.

God is a progressive God. He's always moving forward. By His grace—and with a will determined not to dwell on an unpleasant past—we can overcome the challenge of forgetting those things that are behind. I won't lie to you, it won't be easy. The past may even come back to "haunt" you sometimes. But the battle really is in the mind. The good news is, you have the mind of Christ (1 Cor. 2:16) and God has a good plan for you. Press forward to that goal. Leave the past behind; for good!

Broken Heart Syndrome...

It is one thing to know and plan for the demise of a love one, but it's another to deal with it suddenly. Yes, both are painful and challenging however in my personal experience I felt a little side swiped, a little blind sighted to say the least.

Upon returning from an eight day journey in Israel with a group of women, I was given the news that my mother was struggling to breathe. How could this be when I talk to her all the way to the airport? In my mind I was thinking, it couldn't be that bad, she's always managed to pull through.

I got on the next flight heading home only to find that momma was practically gone. Broken was an understatement. I got as close as I could to share my most inner thoughts as I wept from the depths of my soul." This cannot be," "you didn't even try" I repeatedly shouted. Meanwhile I tried to rub life into her lifeless hands and feet. Finally, I reverted back to a child and climbed into bed with the person that watched me develop and grow while nurturing my unique personality.

Once again, I didn't' allow myself time to grieve and I honestly believed the old saying that time heals all wounds. Therefore, I return back to church on Sunday and work on Monday, all while replaying it, moment by moment. I kept working, serving, grinding and as usual, I kept it moving. Moving so much until I began to stutter when I spoke. My heart was heavy and I didn't feel comfortable enough to share.

It is true that unexpressed grief brings about complex emotional and physical illness. Hence the reason I began to experience anxiety as well as chest pains throughout both day and night. I believed God for everyone else but was in denial that I needed help myself. Yes, a God fearing women that not only needed a release from grief but inner healing from the memory of this devastation.

Eventually I was diagnosed by a cardiologist with anxiety and broken heart syndrome. Although I was in disbelief, I turned to the word of the Lord and recognized that even Jesus himself understood hurt and was acquainted with grief. I have since learned that it takes longer to mend a broken heart if you are not willing to accept the fact that the past is not altered. On the other hand, the perception of what has taken place is nurtured by the mind and will. Keeping your heart and mind pure during determines how *beautiful* you become.

Chapter Eight

God Restores

Even after storms end there are some that leave scars that serve as reminders of the permanent damage left behind.

Imagine the current lives of the parents of the many teenagers who have been gunned downed on the cold, violent streets of Chicago; or the divorce that took place between a couple who had been married for twenty years; or the family who lost their home to foreclosure and are struggling to find shelter for their children; or the child who lost both their parents in a car accident and are forced to live from one foster care home to another; or the elderly man or woman whose body is stricken with cancer; or the toddler who has a terminal disease.

When those types of things happen, you never forget them. You may learn to live through them, but they change you forever. I am certain if you look on your body there are scars that are still there that remind you of a fall you took as a child. While the pain is no longer felt, the scar is there—forever. Even when bones are broken, they may heal, but it is not uncommon to feel an ache or pain ten years later, when it gets cold or rains outside.

But have you ever gone through something so bad you wish the healing process would hurry up and take its course? Have you ever experienced so much pain you thought your heart would literally stop beating?

Tell me, what do you do when you are at a breaking point? When life's winds are blowing so strong you are tossed on every side. When it appears, the violent wind is snuffing out the very breath in your body.

One of my favorite passages of scripture to read during times like that is found in II Corinthians 4:8-9 (KJV).

"We are troubled on every side, yet not distressed; we are perplexed, but not in despair; persecuted, but not forsaken; cast down, but not destroyed."

It picks up in verse 16 saying, *"For which cause we faint not; but though our outward man perish, yet the inward man is renewed day by day. For our light affliction, which is but for a moment, worketh for us a far more exceeding and eternal weight of glory; while we look not at the things which are seen, but at the things which are not seen: for the things which are seen are temporal; but the things which are not seen are eternal."*

The enemy wants you to break because he knows how hard it is for brokenness to heal. Beloved, what I am saying to you is some storms come specifically to break you. The devil is not concerned with you just getting an injury and having to sit out of a game. He is aiming to break you enough to put you out of the game. His goal is to get you so broken and discouraged until you have no strength to persevere.

You've read and heard that the race is not given to the swift or the strong, but to the one who endures to the end. He is not after your start; he is after your finish.

Some of the worst breaking points come after some of your best victories. Ever have a season where it seems everything was going the way you wanted it to go and no sooner than you can get comfortable, mess hits the fan? Imagine getting a job promotion on Friday and then walk into your office on Monday and all of a sudden the entire staff has decided to become your newfound enemies. Consequently, making your job difficult to do or tolerate. Imagine a couple celebrating their wedding anniversary on Saturday and then on Monday morning instead of having breakfast together, they are in their attorney's office filing for divorce. How can that be?

Look below at the text found in I Kings 19:1-7 (KJV).

And Ahab told Jezebel all that Elijah had done, and withal how he had slain all the prophets with the sword. Then Jezebel sent a messenger unto

Elijah, saying, So let the gods do to me, and more also, if I make not thy life as the life of one of them by to morrow about this time. And when he saw that, he arose, and went for his life, and came to Beersheba, which belongeth to Judah, and left his servant there. But he himself went a day's journey into the wilderness, and came and sat down under a juniper tree: and he requested for himself that he might die; and said, It is enough; now, O Lord, take away my life; for I am not better than my fathers. And as he lay and slept under a juniper tree, behold, then an angel touched him, and said unto him, Arise and eat. And he looked, and, behold, there was a cake baked on the coals, and a cruse of water at his head. And he did eat and drink, and laid him down again. And the angel of the Lord came again the second time, and touched him, and said, Arise and eat; because the journey is too great for thee.

If you go back a chapter, you will read how Elijah called fire down from Heaven and it led to the destruction of the prophets of Baal. I don't know how you feel about it, but if the Lord had just shown Himself to me in such a demonstrative way, I would have been on a spiritual high. Yet, Elijah found himself running for his life. Particles of fear and hopelessness slowly infiltrated his mind and spirit, and he found himself exemplifying the classic signs of depression. He isolated himself by leaving his posse, took cover under a juniper tree and went to sleep to try and escape reality and he lost his appetite.

I must interject this to combat the notion that I would have been on a spiritual high if the Lord had shown up for me in the way He showed up for Elijah. I feel a pang of conviction. God just said to me, "How many times have I answered your prayers, yet when something new comes up, you doubt me as if I never did a single thing?" How many times do we testify that God gave us the money to pay our bills, He healed our bodies and He saved our children. He's made a way out of no way; but as soon as troubles arise again, we get spiritual amnesia.

Elijah had just seen what God could do. His relationship and connection with the Lord was proven that day when fire fell from

Heaven. But, how many of you know the enemy will turn up the heat just after you have had an encounter with God? In this case, Jezebel had no power. But sometimes a threat will mask itself as the truth. That is why it is so important to do all you can to protect your thoughts. Spiritual warfare will never cease. The devil will always be after you. And when you are between breaking and breakthrough, hold on to what you know to be true about God. You know if He brought you out once, He can do it again.

The angels visited Elijah once he had mentally given up. They did not come with a deep word. They didn't come with a vial of anointing oil and start slathering it all over his body. They did not lay a single hand on him. They simply brought him some food. It goes back to my earlier point. There are times when practicality is needed and not spirituality. They allowed him to rest after he ate. Basically, they allowed him to bend, but stayed around to make sure he had the nutrients he needed to not break. Food energizes your mind and since the war was in Elijah's mind that is what they focused on because, nothing had actually happened. A simple threat caused him to react the way he did. You know how it is when you think something is going to happen. Elijah had probably already envisioned his funeral services. He probably saw in his mind his own beheading. And again, all because of a threat!

But if you keep reading that text on down to verse ten, the Word of the Lord comes. After Elijah's body had been nourished, it was time for his spirit man to be ministered to. My friends, if you are going to survive life's storms, if you are going to bend and not break, it is imperative for you to allow the Word of God to give life to your spirit. You cannot make it without a Word from the Lord. One word from the Lord can change your very life. It changed Elijah's. Elijah's spirit man stood back up and he got back on the battlefield for the Lord.

The devil's threat drove him away from his ministry, but the Lord's calling on his life pushed him back into it.

The devil's threat caused him to be depressed, but the prophetic assignment recharged him.

The devils' threat sent him into the wilderness, but the Lord's voice got him out.

When he left the desert nothing had changed in his circumstances. He just had a Word. A word will give you strength you never knew you had. A word will lead you to your peace, prosperity and promise.

So, you can serve notice to those who thought it was over for you that you are yet alive. The storm might have caused you to bend but you didn't break. It didn't take you out as it might have been predicted to. In Elijah's case, Jezebel was no match for his Jehovah!

We all know the story of Job. Job was sitting at home one day minding his own business when in a matter of minutes he had lost it all. Children, property, investments...gone. Job is a prime example of one who weathers a storm that bends him but it doesn't break him. Many days he cried, he pouted, he cried out to God wondering what he had done to bring such calamity on his life. His own wife told him to curse God and die. While he did not maintain his demeanor, he maintained his declaration. He says in Job 13:15 "Though he slay me, yet will I trust Him: but I will maintain my own ways before Him." That blessed me right there! Job declares that it does not matter how rough it gets. No matter how the storm was raging in his life, his soul was anchored in the Lord. He declares that even though he lost his property, he did not lose his position in his faith. Can you say that today? Can you stand when the bottom is falling out from underneath your feet? Can you remain encouraged through disappointing situations?

We all know how Job's story ends. God gave him more in the end than what he began with. What blessings are we possibly missing out on because we allow the storm to break us? Strong trees can endure the worst of storms. The wind may cause them to lift their branches and wave to the oncoming force, but they hold on. Beloved, hold on, because your change is going to come!

The devil's goal is to get you to give up just before you cross the finish line. One of his best tactics of doing this is to keep moving the finish line so you fail to see that you're making progress. This is meant to tire you out because he knows that if you ever get the resilience you need to persevere, you will be a force to reckon with. There are a lot of people who could do great damage to the kingdom of darkness, but we will never know who they are for many of them have taken a seat on the sidelines of life. Can you imagine watching a football or basketball game and all of the star players were on the bench? Of course not. I wish I could sit from the seat of God and look at the many Christians across the world who are operating lower than their potential because they've grown weary. I bet there are massive numbers of people who were once on fire for God but the storms of life weighed them down to the point they lost their fire, passion, and zeal.

Child of God, can I encourage you? Galatians 6:9 says, "And let us not be weary in well doing: for in due season we shall reap, if we faint not." The first thing I want you to know is you are doing well. I know things have been hard. I know the road has been tough, but considering all of you've been through, you have done well. The fact that you are still in your right mind and not sitting in the corner of a room the size of a prison cell waiting for medication is a testament of just how well you've done. The fact that you were able to forgive those who hurt you and pray for them in the midst of them doing you wrong is a testament that you've done well. The fact that you find a way to get out of your bed, go to work, care for your family and still serve the Lord, is a testament that you've done well. You know you were supposed to have lost it by now, but the Lord has kept you in perfect peace. No, you may not have made all of the right decisions. You may not have stayed on course, but you kept going and that is enough for me to say, you've done well.

A lot of us give up right before we enter our due season. The Bible clearly tells us that the only way to get what's due to us is to hang on and faint not. How many times do we forfeit our blessings because we give up? How many blessings go unclaimed because we throw in the towel?

Here's what I want you to do. I want you to tap into your spirit and ask God to give you a revival in your spirit. I want you to get into your prayer closet and seek God like never before. The Kingdom of God needs you. I believe there is a prayer warrior inside of you. I believe there is a prophetic word in you that need to come out. I believe that there is a song in your spirit that needs to be heard. Will the real you please, stand up?

You are victorious.

You are more than a conqueror.

As a matter of fact, you need to confess that on a daily basis. Do not allow the enemy to tell you who you are. Do not allow him to suppress and stifle you another day. You are closer to the end of your storm than you realize. Get up, wash your face, and press you way.

Ladies, it's time you let go of the hurt of the past. Do something for yourself. Go and get your hair done again. If you can't grow it, weave it. Get you some make-up, put on your heels and strut with the confidence that you are a winner. More importantly, you are the epitome of an overcomer. That storm really did come to take you out, but my God, you are still here. You survived!

Fellas, stop feeling like a failure. Things may not have turned out like you wanted it to. You may not be financially where you thought you would be by now, but it really is alright. You still have time. Take what you have and make it work. Stop walking around with your head held down. You have no reason at all to be ashamed any longer. You don't have to be defensive either. Your past does not dictate your future. What you did in the days of your youth has long been forgotten by the Lord. He has given you another opportunity, and I ask you, what will you do with it? Put your suit on, get a fresh cut and go back out there and be the king you were created to be. Our families are counting on you brothers, to be the heads of your homes. They are counting on you to be strong and powerful leaders. God left us with the dominion and it is past time that we take our rightful place.

The only failure in life is failing to try again.

I pray this chapter will reignite something within you, my brother and my sister, to get up and give life a try one more time. I believe there is a little something left in you that desire to be excellent and great, but you are afraid. Afraid of disappointment. Afraid to be hurt again. Afraid that it may not work. But, within you is the power of resurrection.

You can get up.

You can start over.

You can try again.

The woman with the issue of blood suffered through this for twelve years. The Bible says she spent all of her money going from one doctor to the next, to the point it practically bankrupts her. But even after twelve years, no health insurance, enduring castigation from the community; when Jesus comes through her town holding a crusade, she finds the strength to get up, get dressed and make her way to him. She had no idea if He could help her or if she would even get to Him, but she tried anyway. She left home not knowing what she would encounter. She left home not knowing if she would be stopped.

As she made her way, she had to press through the other people who were falling at his feet.

She had to make her way past the people who were surrounding Him seeking their own miracles. She did not care where He was on His way to; she just knew that she was in need of a miracle. Her need for a miracle was greater than any desire she may have had to stay in her place of desperation. I am sure the voices in her head mocked her as she got dressed. Mocked her as she walked out of the door and saw the swarm of people trying to get his attention. But, in spite of it all, we all know she got her healing after having touched the hem of the Master's garment.

How desperate are you to make it to the Master? How driven are you to get what God has promised you? How determined are you to keep going to see what the end is going to bring?

I cannot promise you will not face anymore trials.

I wish I could tell you that you've jumped your last hurdle. But, I cannot.

I cannot promise you've cried your last tear.

But, here is what I can tell you.

I can tell you your latter will be greater than your former.

I can tell you your best days are ahead of you.

I can tell you God is going to restore to you what the enemy thought he got away with.

So hold on, dear soldier. Don't you dare give up, don't you dare give in. You have come too far to give up now!

The rainbow comes after a storm and shows off all the beautiful colors of the spectrum at once. In the Bible, when a rainbow appeared it was a sign of covenant, a reminder, between God and man. The fact that the rainbow is present means the storm is over, and I'm inclined to prophetically believe that at the time you are reading this book, your unresolved hurt from the past, and the broken pieces of your life are being healed and coming back together again!

Conclusion

One of the most encouraging Scriptures in the Bible is 2 Corinthians 4:7: "But we have this treasure in earthen vessels, that the excellency of the power may be of God, and not of us." Then Paul goes on to describe those earthen vessels dying men, troubled on every side, perplexed, persecuted, cast down. And even though never forsaken or in despair, those men used by God are constantly groaning under the burden of their bodies, waiting anxiously to be clothed with new ones.

God mocks man's power. He laughs at our egotistical efforts at being good. He never uses the high and mighty but, instead, uses the weak things of this world to confound the wise.

"For ye see your calling, brethren, how that not many wise men after the flesh, not many mighty, not many noble, are called: But God hath chose the foolish things of the world to confound the wise; and God hath chose the weak things of the world to confound the things that are mighty; And the base things of the world, and things which are despised, hath God

chosen, yea, and things which are not... That no flesh should glory in his presence" (1 Corinthians 1:26-31).

Wow!

Weak thing, foolish thing, despised thing, abase thing, not very noble, not very smart, nor very mighty. What insanity to think God could use such a person yet, that is His perfect plan, the greatest mystery on earth. God calls us in our weakness, in our brokenness, even when He knows we'll do it wrong. He puts His priceless treasure in these earthen vessels of ours because He delights in doing the impossible with nothing.

Gideon is an example of a called man who had too much going for him. He was called to deliver God's children from slavery. What does he do? He blasts the trumpets and calls together a mighty army. Thousands of valiant fighting men rallied under his banner. But God said to Gideon, "Your army is too great, too many men and too much strength. Send them back! If you win the victory with all this show of strength, you and your people might think you won on your own abilities. You've got too much going for you and I don't want you to steal the glory. Strip down your army!"

One by one, those men leave Gideon's army. He must have stood by thinking, "How ridiculous! Win by weakening ourselves? God calls me to do battle, then asks me to disarm! Insanity! This is the craziest thing God has yet asked me to do. There goes my plan to become a legend in my own time."

Those fighters must have left the battlefield shuddering with astonishment. Who ever heard of winning a battle by laying aside weapons and manpower?

From a human standpoint, it is crazy. Great victories by tiny remnants. Walls tumble without a shot fired. Armies put to flight by a motley orchestra of trumpet players. By the power of faith alone; weak and broken people confound the world.

I will leave you by telling you that brokenness is the path to blessing. Before God can use a man greatly, He must break him, because we all have a built in propensity to trust in ourselves. Brokenness reveals to us the power of our God.

God blesses us as we cling to Him in our brokenness. Often our greatest victories come out of the ashes of our greatest defeats. Recall the story of Jacob? Well, as soon as Jacob was crippled, he was able to hang on to the Lord for dear life. He knew now that if God didn't bless him, he had no hope. He couldn't trust in himself any longer, because he was crippled. He had to cling to the Lord and in clinging to the Lord in his brokenness; Jacob received the blessing he had been scheming to get all his life.

There's a paradox here, in that Jacob seems to have incredible strength in clinging to the Lord after he is wounded. Of course, the Lord could have loosened Jacob's grip and gotten away. But the Lord loves it when His children cling to Him in their brokenness and say, "I won't let You go until You bless me."

What am I saying?

Being broken is sometimes the best thing that can happen to you. You may have started this book thinking it was the worst thing ever. But, I hope by now you have received some inspiration that will result in you taking your broken pieces and making something great with them.

Something new.

Something more beautiful than what you had before.

Because although broken, broken pieces still have value. No, seriously. I need you to know you are extremely valuable. You are worth more than millions, even billions. You are priceless. Everything you have been through up until this moment has been for a purpose—a cause. A purpose so great that even your imagination fails to comprehend. A purpose so great that it fails to compare to all you have had to go through to get to it.

If you are locked in what seems like a never-ending trial, just remember it's part of your process. At some point, God is going to reach into the fire and take you out. Did you know that a refiner of silver has to keep his eye on the silver at all times so as to not burn it? If kept one second longer than it's supposed to be in the fire, it'll burn. So, the silversmith has to watch it and he knows it's ready when he can look over at the silver and see his reflection. My God! Don't you know that if a silversmith takes that much care with silver, your Heavenly Father is sure to take even better care of you? When he looks at you and can see His reflection, then He will take you out and present you for the entire world to see.

Take comfort in knowing that you are never not under the watchful eye of the Almighty!

About the Author

Teacher, Psalmist, Visionary, and most of all Servant Girl. These words best describe the path in which Pastor Kenya L. May navigates through life. Born in Chicago, Illinois to Mr. and Mrs. Chester L. Gavin, she has been ordained since birth to live her life on purpose on assignment from God.

Pastor Kenya graduated from Covert Public School and later matriculated to college. She earned a Bachelor's Degree in Elementary Education from Western Michigan University and a Master's Degree in Organizational Management from Virginia Lynchburg University. Currently she is a 4th grade teacher with Charlotte Mecklenburg Schools. Through instruction and training she has been able to implement educational programs within the children's ministry at her local church.

Pastor Kenya is happily united to her childhood sweetheart, Bishop Amere J. May, Sr who is the senior pastor of Abundant Faith Word Church located in Charlotte, North Carolina. She is the proud mother of three children and four grandchildren. While expanding her ministry, she has learned to expertly balance her career, ministry and family.

Passionate about living a life of purpose, Pastor Kenya serves as the as the Administrative Pastor of Abundant Faith Word Church in the city of Charlotte, North Carolina. This multi-talented vessel of God has implemented many spiritual gifts within the Body of Christ. It is a true saying that powerful things come in small packages. She truly has a Pastor's heart and makes herself available as a mentor and source of strength restoring the joy of the women that have been physically, sexually and verbally abused. For that reason, Pastor May has made a dramatic impact on the women at Abundant Faith Word Church, by sharing the truest version of herself.

Pastor Kenya is best known for being an anointed prophetic psalmist. She ministers in song until the glory of God fills the room. She has a prophetic voice that has change the lives of both men and women across America. She has been blessed to record her freshman CD "I'm Coming Out".

With dynamic wisdom and humility, Pastor Kenya May has boldly accepted God's call to leadership. Through her close relationship with him, she has claimed her ultimate purpose. To live life with him, aMAYzingly!